World Book, Inc.
180 North LaSalle Street
Suite 900
Chicago, Illinois 60601
USA

For information about other "True or False?" titles, as
well as other World Book print and digital publications,
please go to www.worldbook.com.

For information about other World Book publications,
call 1-800-WORLDBK (967-5325).

For information about sales to schools and libraries,
call 1-800-975-3250 (United States) or 1-800-837-5365
(Canada).

Library of Congress Cataloging-in-Publication Data for
this volume has been applied for.

True or False?
ISBN: 978-0-7166-3725-7 (set, hc.)

Inventions
ISBN: 978-0-7166-3729-5 (hc.)

Also available as:
ISBN: 978-0-7166-3739-4 (e-book)

Printed in China by Shenzhen Wing King Tong Paper
Products Co., Ltd., Shenzhen, Guangdong
1st printing July 2018

Staff

Executive Committee

President
Jim O'Rourke

Vice President and
Editor in Chief
Paul A. Kobasa

Vice President, Finance
Donald D. Keller

Vice President, Marketing
Jean Lin

Vice President, International
Maksim Rutenberg

Vice President, Technology
Jason Dole

Director, Human Resources
Bev Ecker

Editorial

Director, New Print
Tom Evans

Writer
Grace Guibert

Managing Editor
Jeff De La Rosa

Librarian
S. Thomas Richardson

Manager, Contracts and
Compliance
(Rights and Permissions)
Loranne K. Shields

Manager, Indexing Services
David Pofelski

Digital

Director, Digital Product
Development
Erika Meller

Digital Product Manager
Jonathan Wills

Manufacturing/Production

Manufacturing Manager
Anne Fritzinger

Production Specialist
Curley Hunter

Proofreader
Nathalie Strassheim

Graphics and Design

Senior Art Director
Tom Evans

Senior Visual
Communications Designer
Melanie Bender

Senior Designer
Isaiah Sheppard

Media Editor
Rosalia Bledsoe

INVENTIONS

WORLD BOOK

www.worldbook.com

Only scientists and
engineers invent things.

An invention is any tool, machine, or way to do something that solves a problem, makes work easier, or makes life better. All sorts of people—even kids—have had ideas that turned into famous inventions!

All inventions are made after lots of thought, hard work, and careful planning.

Many inventors stumble upon their inventions by chance. For example, the Slinky was invented when an engineer knocked over a spring and liked the way it moved.

You can be paid for your invention in chocolate.

You wouldn't be the first! The inventor of the chocolate chip cookie, Ruth Wakefield, sold her recipe to the Nestlé company for a lifetime supply of chocolate.

Inventor Mary B. Shrink invented a shrink ray that can make people bug-sized.

SHRINK RAY MACHINE

17

Outside of science fiction, shrink rays have not been invented. Scientists say that it is not possible to shrink people because some parts of our bodies would not work if they were made small.

 18

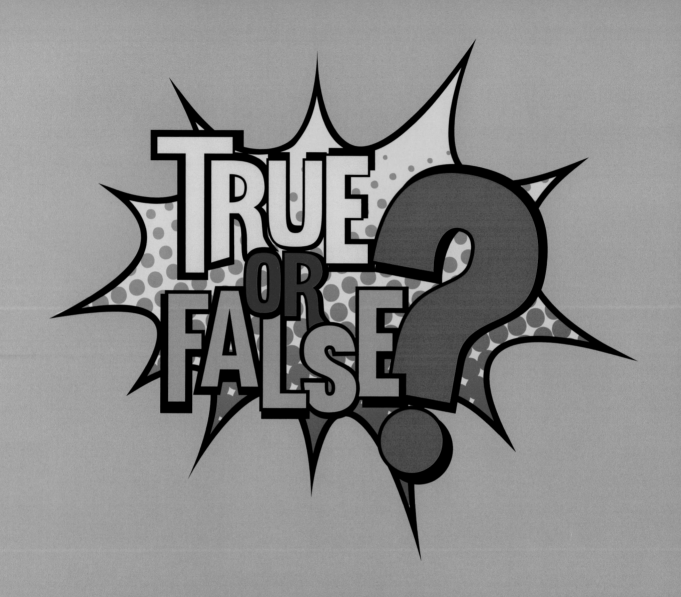

A dog helped invent Velcro.

TRUE!

Swiss engineer Georges de Mestral got the idea for Velcro in the 1940's when he saw burs stuck in his dog's fur. Velcro works like burs. Tiny hooks catch tiny loops to fasten materials together.

A patent helps inventors own their inventions.

Patents are given by the government. They give inventors the right to stop others from making, selling, or copying their inventions.

You cannot patent living things.

In 1988, the United States government gave a patent for an animal. It was given to scientists who changed mice to help study the disease called cancer. These mice glowed in the dark!

The can and the can opener were invented at the same time.

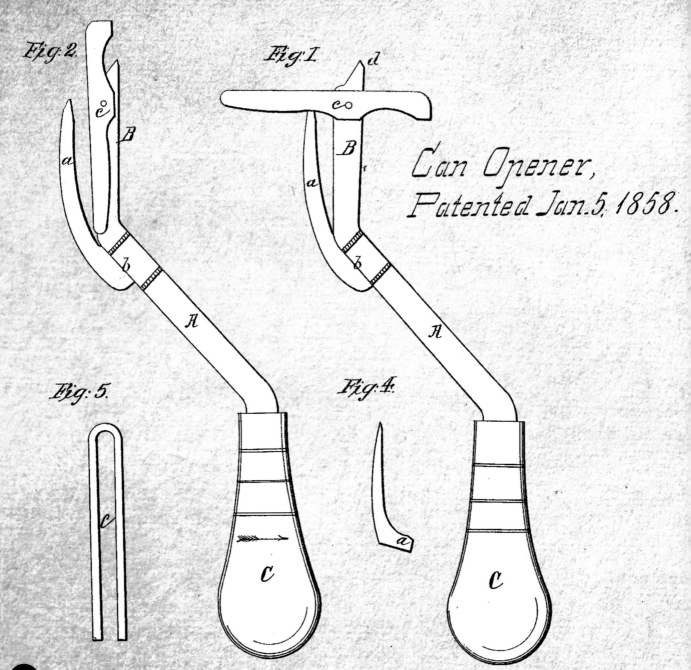

Fig. 2.   Fig. 1.   Can Opener,
Patented Jan. 5, 1858.

Fig. 5.   Fig. 4.

The can opener was invented almost 50 years after the can. Before the can opener, people opened cans with a hammer and a chisel!

TRUE OR FALSE?

BubbleWrap was
invented to be wallpaper.

The inventors of BubbleWrap wanted to make three-dimensional wallpaper. Bubble wallpaper was not popular. But it has turned out to be good packing material!

TRUE OR FALSE?

Inventors have always gotten credit for their inventions.

Throughout history, women and people of color have faced discrimination. This means that people treated them unfairly because of their differences. In the United States and Europe, it used to be hard for women or people of color to get credit for their ideas.

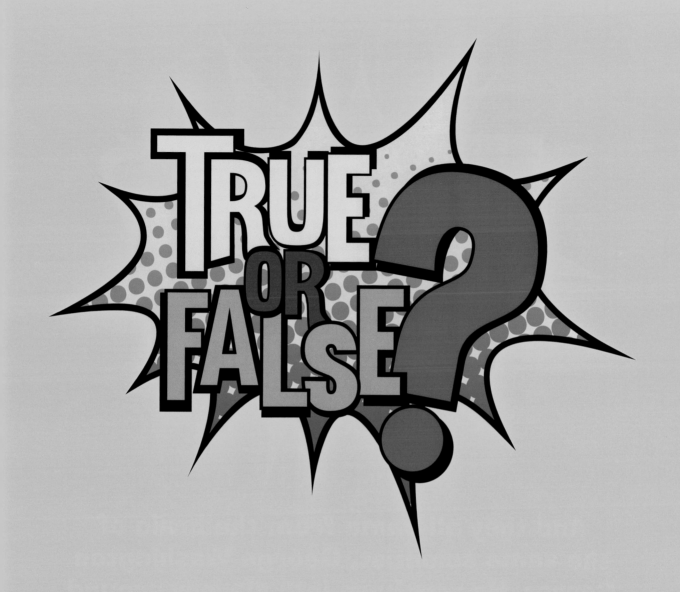

There are more than 300 invented uses for peanuts.

TRUE!

And they all came from the brain of the same scientist, George Washington Carver. He was born into slavery around 1864. Some of the products made from peanuts that he invented are soap, ink, face powder, and a milk substitute.

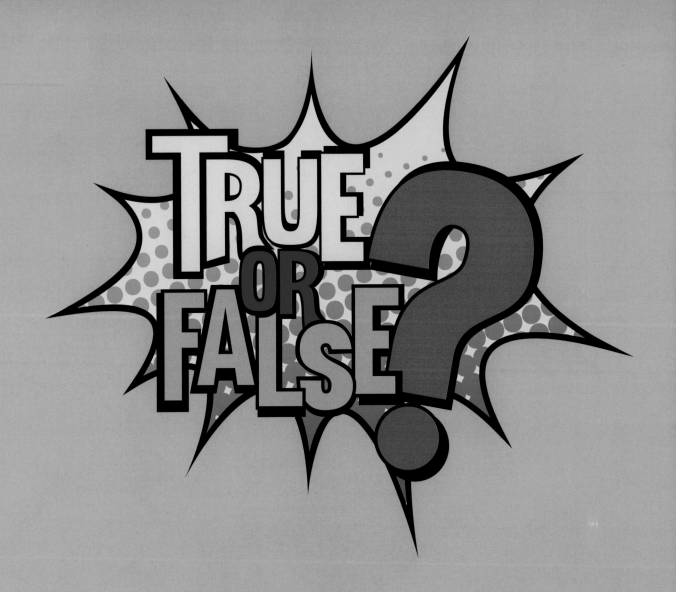

Chewing gum was invented by people living thousands of years ago in the country now called Greece.

A

B

1

4

5

6

50

The ancient Greeks chewed gum made from the bark of the mastic tree. The kind of chewing gum we have today was invented much later, in the 1860's.

People invent things to become rich and famous.

People who invent things might get rich, but the main reason for invention is to help others. An invention must be or do something people want. If an invention does not help people, it will not succeed.

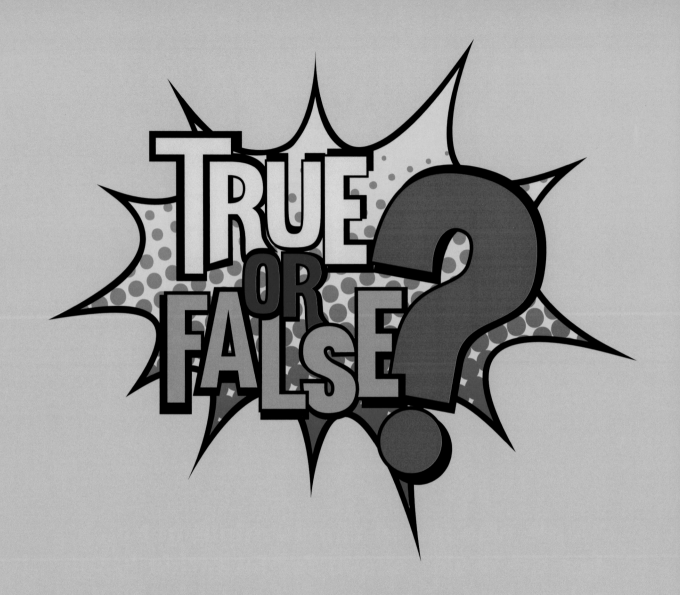

Play-Doh was invented to be a cleaning product.

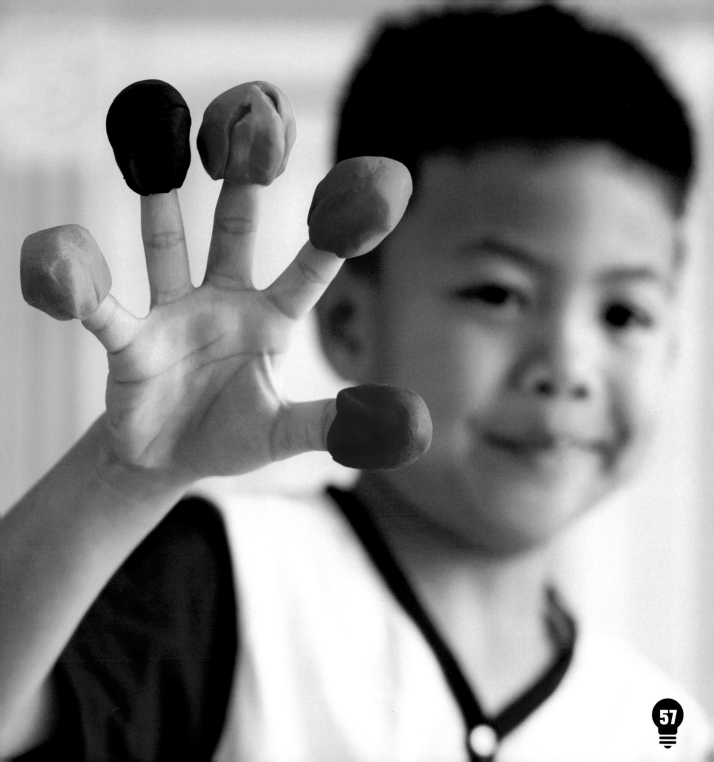

The sticky, squishy modeling clay was originally meant to be used to clean wallpaper! Sometimes inventions have more than one use.

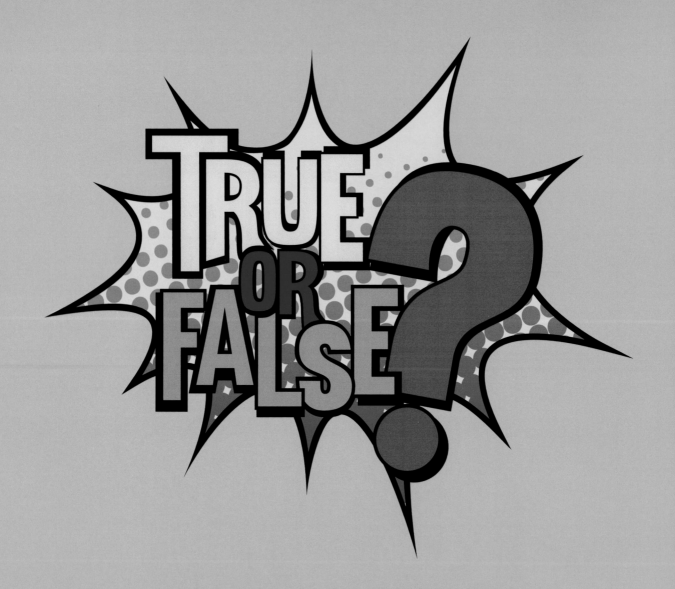

All inventions are modern, technological, and complicated.

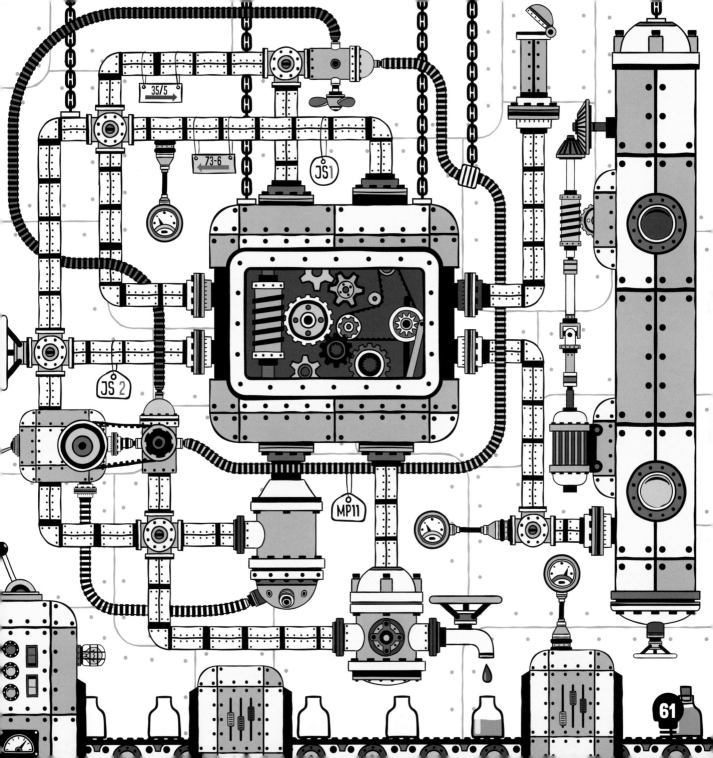

People have invented things as long as there have been people—that is a very long time! The plow and the wheel were invented more than 5,000 years ago. Paper was invented about 2,000 years ago. Even the most simple things we use today had to be invented at some point!

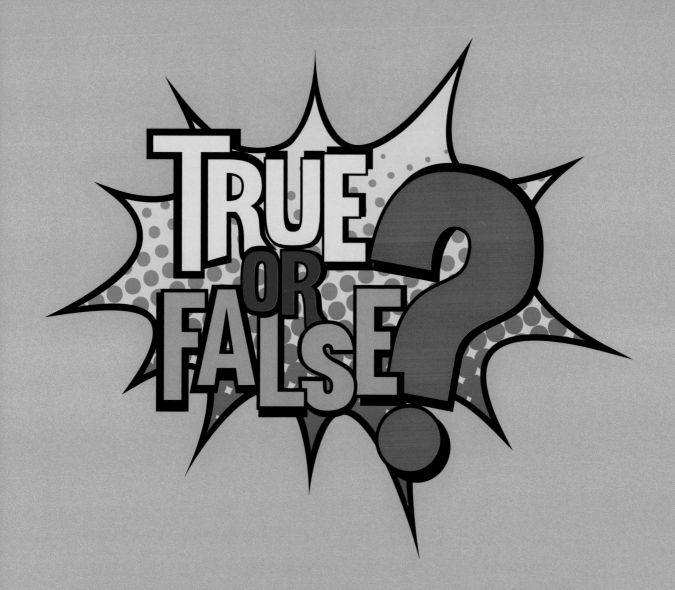

The inventor Alexander Graham Bell is famous for creating the graham cracker.

Alexander Graham Bell is best known for inventing the telephone. The graham cracker is named for Sylvester Graham, an American who taught about healthy food in the early 1800's.

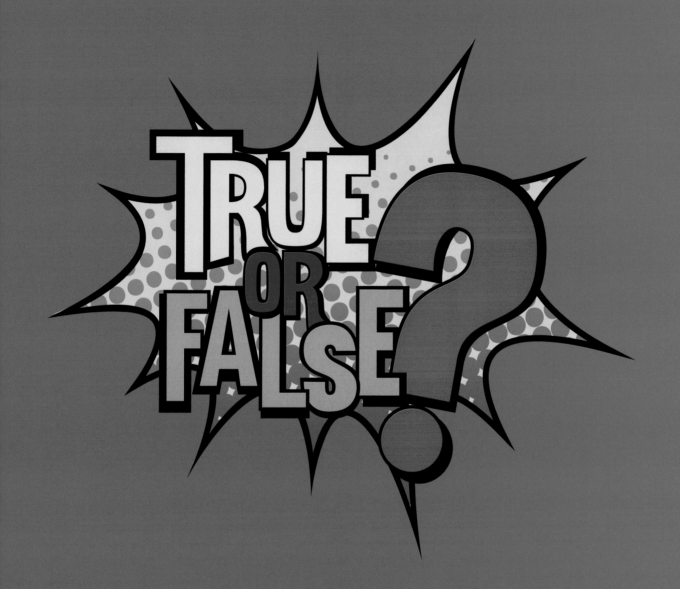

Wild animals also invent things.

Scientists have discovered that apes, crows, and some other animals make tools. For example, chimpanzees use sticks or long blades of grass to poke around termite mounds and anthills to catch the insects for food.

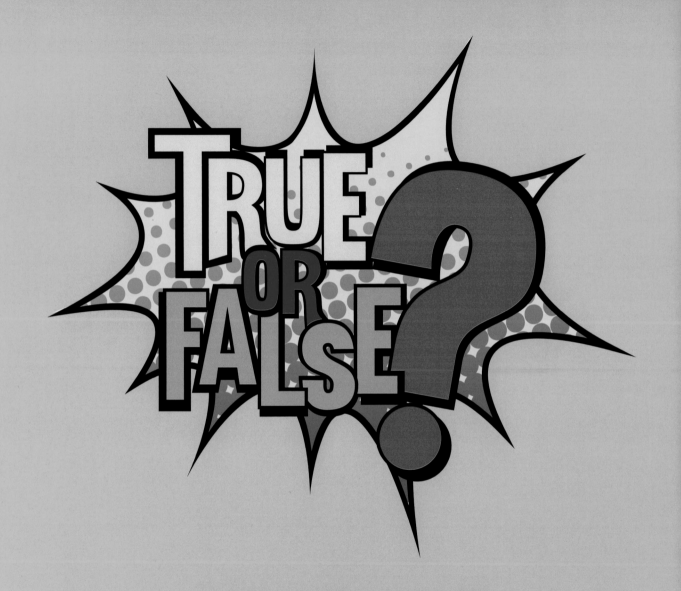

A dentist invented the
cotton candy machine.

Fairy Floss

In 1897, a dentist named William Morrison and a candy maker named John C. Wharton created a machine to make fluffy candy from sugar and flavoring. Cotton candy was originally called Fairy Floss. Today, dentists say skip the sweets, brush twice a day, and use dental floss!

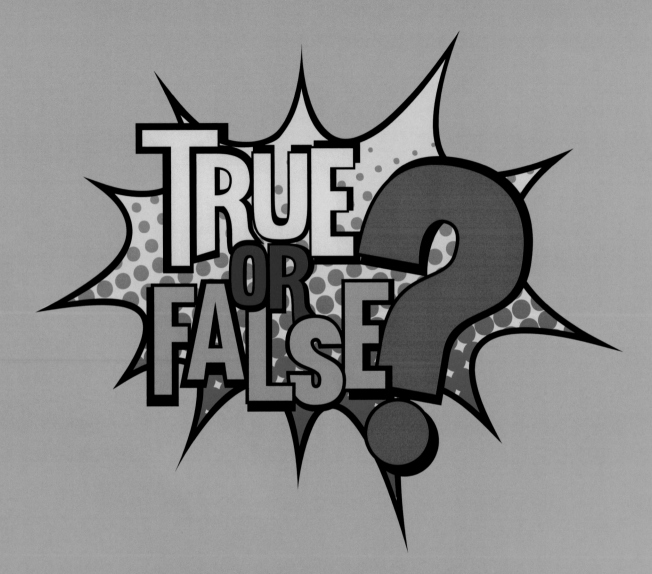

Thomas Edison, one of the greatest inventors in history, received thousands of patents.

Edison was given 1,093 patents by the United States government alone! He received thousands of patents from governments around the world. Edison worked on the phonograph, the light bulb, and motion pictures. Some of Edison's patents were received for his own inventions. Others were for things that people developed in his laboratories.

Frisbees are named after their inventor, Felicity Frisbee.

The name Frisbee comes from the Frisbie Pie Company in Connecticut, USA. The Frisbie Pie Company sold pies to college students at Yale University. Students would toss around the empty pie tins just like today's Frisbees!

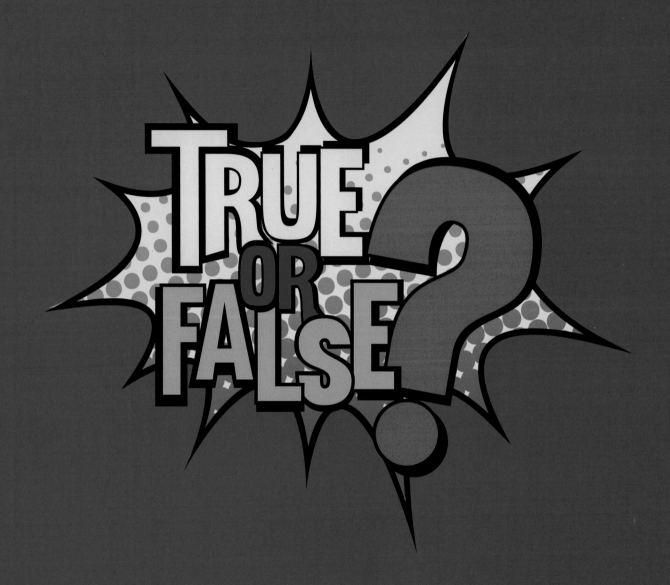

TRUE OR FALSE?

Inventions can save lives.

84

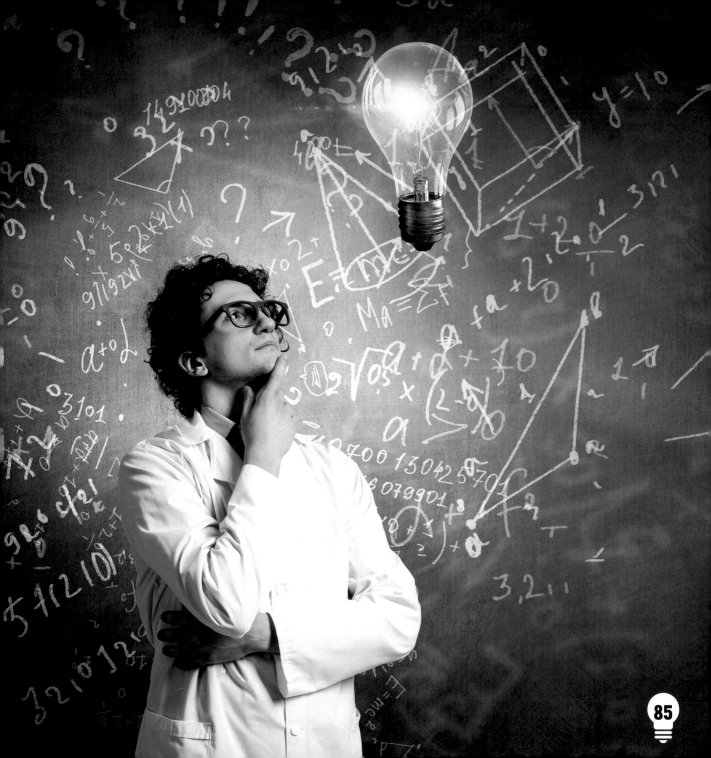

Some of the most important inventions have saved thousands of lives. Before some kinds of medicine were invented, people died from sicknesses we can cure today. Scientists try to make new and better medicines all the time.

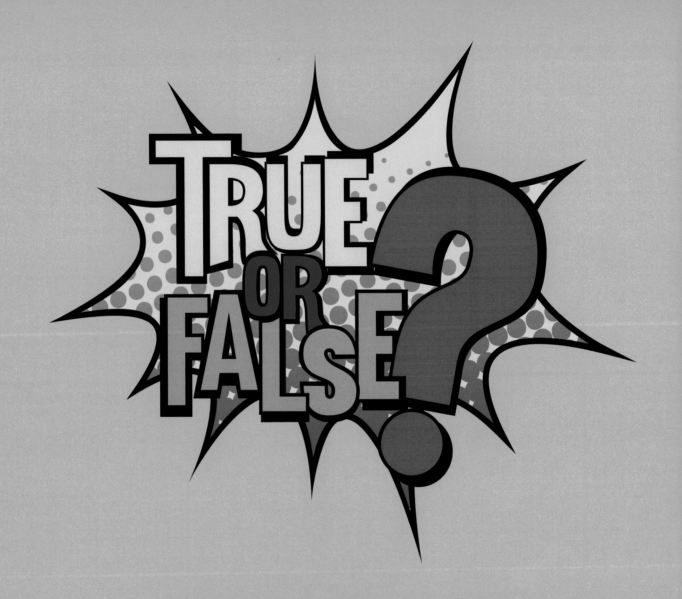

**Discoveries and inventions
are the same things.**

A discovery is seeing something in nature for the first time. An invention is making something for the first time. For example, people discovered fire, but they invented the match to start a fire.

Which exciting thing will you discover or invent?

91

DID YOU KNOW...

The **high five** wasn't invented until the 1970's.

Telescopes were invented by accident!

Popsicles were originally called **Eppsicles!** They were named after their inventor, Frank Epperson.

Bagpipes are a famous symbol of Scotland. But they were invented in the **Middle East!**

The recipe for **Coca-Cola** isn't patented...

Alexander Graham Bell wanted people to answer the telephone by saying **"Ahoy!"** instead of **"Hello."**

"Ahoy!"

It took **30 years** for inventor Gordon Gould to patent the **laser.**

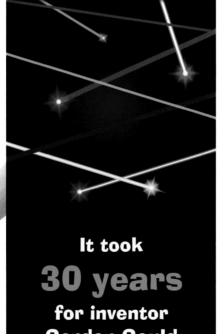

...but nobody outside the company **can figure it out!**

Index

Acknowledgments

Cover: © Alexander Lysenko, Shutterstock; © Exo Pixel/Shutterstock; © Linear Test Pilot/Shutterstock

5-9 © Shutterstock

10 Slinky® is a registered trademark of Alex Brands; © Richard Watkins, Alamy Images

13 © Dmitriy Saveliev, Shutterstock

14-15 Nestlé® is a registered trademark; © Shutterstock; © INTERFOTO/Alamy Images

16-19 WORLD BOOK illustration by Matt Carrington

21 Velcro® is a registered trademark; © Shutterstock

22 © Albert Lleal, Minden Pictures/SuperStock

25 © Rawpixel.com/Shutterstock

26 © Bill Oxford, iStockphoto

28 © Shutterstock

31 © KK/AP Photo

33 © Shutterstock

34 United States Patent and Trademark Office

37-39 BubbleWrap® is a registered trademark of Sealed Air; © Shutterstock

40-44 © Shutterstock

47 Library of Congress; © Shutterstock

49 © Shutterstock

50 Public Domain

53-57 © Shutterstock

58 Play-Doh® is a registered trademark of Hasbro; © Everett Collection/Shutterstock

61-63 © Shutterstock

64 Library of Congress; © Brent Hofacker, Shutterstock

67 Library of Congress

68-71 © Steve Bloom Images/SuperStock

73-75 © Shutterstock

77 Library of Congress

79 © Apic/Getty Images

80 © Bettmann/Getty Images

83 Photos Courtesy of Dan O'Connor, Frisbie Pie Company

85-91 © Shutterstock

92 Popsicles® is a registered trademark of Unilever; © Shutterstock

93 Coca-Cola™ is a trademark of The Coca-Cola Company; © Shutterstock